Who Took the Teacher's Scissors?

Written by Jade Michaels

Illustrated by Dave Gunson

"Who took my scissors?"
said the teacher.
"Did you take them, Chimpanzee?"

"No, I did not take your scissors,"
said Chimpanzee.
"I was swinging in the tree
with Monkey."

3

"Did you take my scissors, Tiger?" said the teacher.

"No," said Tiger. "I did not take your scissors.
I was running in the grass with Cheetah."

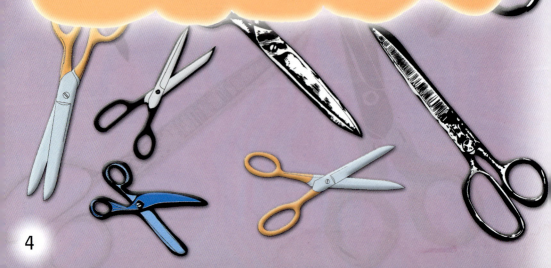

"Did you take my scissors?"
the teacher said to Hippo.

"No, I did not," said Hippo.
"I was swimming in the water
with Seal. I did not
take your scissors."

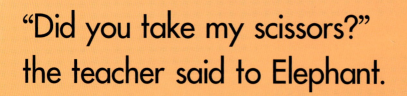

"Did you take my scissors?"
the teacher said to Elephant.

"No," said Elephant.
"I was playing with Zebra.
I did not take your scissors."

"Did you take my scissors, Camel?" said the teacher.

"No," said Camel. "Snake and I were playing in the sand."

11

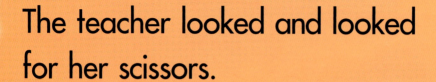

The teacher looked and looked
for her scissors.

"Well, if it was not you,
who took my scissors?"
she said. "Who was it?"

"I can see who took your scissors," said Giraffe.
"Look up there in the tree.
Look in that nest."

"Crow took your scissors."